C000004756

PARISH
SUNDAY VESPERS

Evening Prayer with Benediction
for Parishes

Edited by Michael Beattie SJ

COLLINS

About This Book

The Second Vatican Council heralded a much-needed renovation of the way in which we worship in public. Many of the principles outlined by Pope Pius XII in his encyclical letter *Mediator Dei* were implemented in the Council's Constitution on the Liturgy. Almost twenty years after that Constitution, and approaching forty years after the encyclical, we have become accustomed to celebrating Mass in English. We are encouraged to be real participants and not mere bystanders.

The Divine Office, or Breviary or Prayer of the Church, has also been translated into English; and what was once a 'closed book' is now used for daily prayer not only by priests and religious but also by many lay people. The recently-revised rite for the worship of the Blessed Sacrament outside Mass, which allows for part of the Liturgy of the Hours to be recited during Exposition of the Blessed Sacrament, has given a wonderful opportunity for parishes to develop a form of evening service consisting of Vespers, or the Evening Prayer of the Church, recited or sung before the Blessed Sacrament and integrated with Benediction.

Many Catholics today feel that there is a real need for some form of devotion in church which includes time for communal prayer, reflection and silence. Vespers and Benediction seem to meet this need. This is borne out by the high attendance week by week at the Sacred Heart Church in Wimbledon. Older parishioners remark on the fact that attendance is higher than in days gone by when, before Vatican II and the advent of evening Mass, there were the traditional services and Benediction.

Why is the attendance high? Several reasons can be given. Firstly, a realisation that the Divine Office is the official prayer of the Church. The Council explicitly tells us that Christ continues his priestly work through the Church not only in the celebration of Mass but also in the recitation of the Divine Office. Secondly, the planning of this little book necessitates total congregational participation. Thirdly, the arrangement of hymns, psalms, scripture and prayer, together with periods of silence to be found in the Divine Office, all before the Blessed Sacrament, fulfils a deep-felt need for personal prayer and reflection as a praying community. Fourthly, the time of the service is most important. In Wimbledon, we start off with Exposition of the Blessed Sacrament at 3.30 pm and proceed to sing Vespers at 4.15. This seems more popular than the traditional later time for evening service.

It is with all this in mind that this book of Sunday Evening Prayer of the Church has been prepared. It is the fruit of actual experience — its forerunner being a hand-printed brochure. Exact texts from *The Divine Office* are to be found in this book but there are also versions which vary in minute translation of detail in order to allow the congregation to sing them to well-loved and well-tried tunes. An example would be the several versions of the Magnificat. The musical settings of the psalms are adaptations of Anglican psalmody. Either the congregation can sing in unison, 'left-hand side versus right-hand side', or a cantor can alternate with the whole congregation throughout. We have found the latter to be more effective. For the Short Responsory, verses have been chosen mostly from familiar hymns which express a suitable prayer after silent reflection on scripture. The numeration of items is designed to make handling of the book easy during the service; and the use of flashcards — HYMN: PSALMS: CANTICLE: WORD OF GOD: MAGNIFICAT: HYMN: — on the hymnboard will likewise make for uncomplicated and smooth running of the service. Producing the flashcards, and perhaps one or two new hymnboards with six long slots rather than the usual four or five short ones, can involve the talents of one or more parishioners. The book should be used in conjunction with your parish hymn book for the opening and recessional hymns. The full accompaniments for all other parts of the service are included here for the convenience of the organist.

It is hoped that this little volume, which the Sacred Heart Church finds so valuable, will fulfil a real need in many other parishes. I am grateful for the help given by Mrs Anne Coombs, Mrs Christine Cleverdon and Father E. Warner SJ, and by the Ursuline Sisters in Wimbledon in the early preparation of this book.

Sacred Heart Church   Michael Beattie SJ
Wimbledon   April 1982

Introduction

1

PLEASE STAND

Everyone makes the sign of the cross as the celebrant sings:

or:

O God, come to our aid.   O God, come to our aid.

ALL O Lord, make haste to help us.   Glory be to the Father,

and to the Son, and to the Ho - ly Spi - rit,   as it was in the beginning,

* *outside Lent:*

is now, and ever shall be, world with-out end. A - men. Al - le - lu - ia.

* *in Lent:*

is now, and ev - er shall be, world with - out end. A - men.

Hymn

(the first number on the board)

The Blessed Sacrament is exposed and incensed during the singing of the hymn.
PLEASE SIT for the psalms and the canticle.

2

Psalm 109

ANTIPHON (recited before and after the psalm). A selection of texts will be found on p. 49.

1 The Lord's revelation to my Master: 'Sit ON MY RIGHT:
2 A prince from the day of your birth on the HO - LY MOUNTAINS;
3 The Master standing at YOUR RIGHT HAND:
4 Glory be to the Father, and TO THE SON,

1 your foes I will put be - NEATH YOUR FEET.'
2 from the womb before the dawn I BE - GOT YOU.
3 will shatter kings in the day OF HIS WRATH.
4 and to the HO - LY SPIRIT,

1 The Lord will wield from Sion your scep - TRE OF POWER:
2 The Lord has sworn an oath he will not change;† 'You are a PRIEST FOR EVER,
3 He shall drink from the stream BY THE WAYSIDE
4 as it was in the beginning, is now, and E - VER SHALL BE,

1 rule in the midst of ALL YOUR FOES.
2 a priest like Melchize - DEK OF OLD.'
3 and therefore he shall lift UP HIS HEAD.
4 world without END. A - MEN.

Psalm 109

ANTIPHON (recited before and after the psalm). A selection of texts will be found on p. 49.

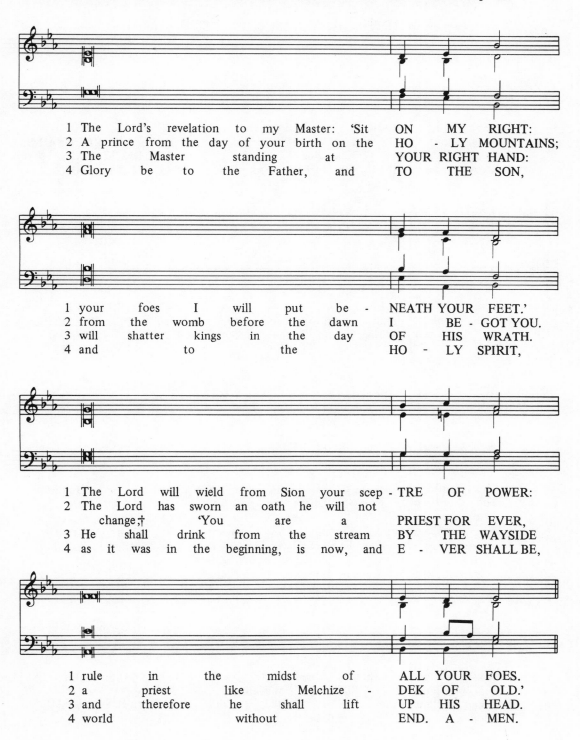

1 The Lord's revelation to my Master: 'Sit ON MY RIGHT:
2 A prince from the day of your birth on the HO - LY MOUNTAINS;
3 The Master standing at YOUR RIGHT HAND:
4 Glory be to the Father, and TO THE SON,

1 your foes I will put be - NEATH YOUR FEET.'
2 from the womb before the dawn I BE - GOT YOU.
3 will shatter kings in the day OF HIS WRATH.
4 and to the HO - LY SPIRIT,

1 The Lord will wield from Sion your scep - TRE OF POWER:
2 The Lord has sworn an oath he will not change;† 'You are a PRIEST FOR EVER,
3 He shall drink from the stream BY THE WAYSIDE
4 as it was in the beginning, is now, and E - VER SHALL BE,

1 rule in the midst of ALL YOUR FOES.
2 a priest like Melchize - DEK OF OLD.'
3 and therefore he shall lift UP HIS HEAD.
4 world without END. A - MEN.

4

Psalm 109

ANTIPHON (recited before and after the psalm). A selection of texts will be found on p. 49.

1 The Lord's revelation to my Master: 'Sit ON MY RIGHT:
2 A prince from the day of your birth on the HO - LY MOUNTAINS;
3 The Master standing at YOUR RIGHT HAND:
4 Glory be to the Father, and TO THE SON,

1 your foes I will put be - NEATH YOUR FEET.'
2 from the womb before the dawn I BE - GOT YOU.
3 will shatter kings in the day OF HIS WRATH.
4 and to the HO - LY SPIRIT,

1 The Lord will wield from Sion your scep - TRE OF POWER:
2 The Lord has sworn an oath he will not
change;† 'You are a PRIEST FOR EVER,
3 He shall drink from the stream BY THE WAYSIDE
4 as it was in the beginning, is now, and E - VER SHALL BE,

1 rule in the midst of ALL YOUR FOES.
2 a priest like Melchize - DEK OF OLD.'
3 and therefore he shall lift UP HIS HEAD.
4 world without END. A - MEN.

Psalm 109

ANTIPHON (recited before and after the psalm). A selection of texts will be found on p. 49.

1 The Lord's revelation to my Master: 'Sit ON MY RIGHT:
2 A prince from the day of your birth on the HO - LY MOUNTAINS;
3 The Master standing at YOUR RIGHT HAND:
4 Glory be to the Father, and TO THE SON,

1 your foes I will put be - NEATH YOUR FEET.'
2 from the womb before the dawn I BE - GOT YOU.
3 will shatter kings in the day OF HIS WRATH.
4 and to the HO - LY SPIRIT,

1 The Lord will wield from Sion your scep - TRE OF POWER:
2 The Lord has sworn an oath he will not change;† 'You are a PRIEST FOR EVER,
3 He shall drink from the stream BY THE WAYSIDE
4 as it was in the beginning, is now, and E - VER SHALL BE,

1 rule in the midst of ALL YOUR FOES.
2 a priest like Melchize - DEK OF OLD.'
3 and therefore he shall lift UP HIS HEAD.
4 world without END. A - MEN.

7

ANTIPHON (recited before and after the psalm). A selection of texts will be found on p. 49.

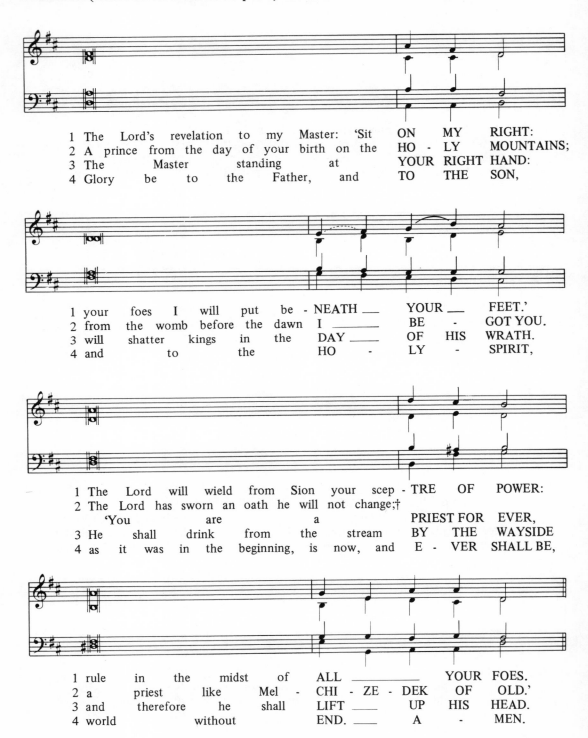

1 The Lord's revelation to my Master: 'Sit ON MY RIGHT:
2 A prince from the day of your birth on the HO - LY MOUNTAINS;
3 The Master standing at YOUR RIGHT HAND:
4 Glory be to the Father, and TO THE SON,

1 your foes I will put be - NEATH ___ YOUR ___ FEET.'
2 from the womb before the dawn I ___ BE - GOT YOU.
3 will shatter kings in the DAY ___ OF HIS WRATH.
4 and to the HO - LY - SPIRIT,

1 The Lord will wield from Sion your scep - TRE OF POWER:
2 The Lord has sworn an oath he will not change;†
   'You are a PRIEST FOR EVER,
3 He shall drink from the stream BY THE WAYSIDE
4 as it was in the beginning, is now, and E - VER SHALL BE,

1 rule in the midst of ALL ___ YOUR FOES.
2 a priest like Mel - CHI - ZE - DEK OF OLD.'
3 and therefore he shall LIFT ___ UP HIS HEAD.
4 world without END. ___ A - MEN.

Psalm 109

ANTIPHON (recited before and after the psalm). A selection of texts will be found on p. 49.

1 The Lord's revelation to my Master: 'Sit ON MY RIGHT:
2 A prince from the day of your birth on the HO - LY MOUNTAINS;
3 The Master standing at YOUR RIGHT HAND:
4 Glory be to the Father, and TO THE SON,

1 your foes I will put be - NEATH __ YOUR __ FEET.'
2 from the womb before the dawn I __ BE - GOT YOU.
3 will shatter kings in the DAY __ OF HIS WRATH.
4 and to the HO - LY - SPIRIT,

1 The Lord will wield from Sion your scep - TRE OF POWER:
2 The Lord has sworn an oath he will not change;†
   'You are a PRIEST FOR EVER,
3 He shall drink from the stream BY THE WAYSIDE
4 as it was in the beginning, is now, and E - VER SHALL BE,

1 rule in the midst of ALL __ YOUR FOES.
2 a priest like Mel - CHI - ZE - DEK OF OLD.'
3 and therefore he shall LIFT __ UP HIS HEAD.
4 world without END. __ A - MEN.

ANTIPHON (recited before and after the psalm). A selection of texts will be found on p. 50.

```
1 When        Israel        came              FORTH FROM EGYPT,
2 The          sea          fled              AT    THE   SIGHT:
3 Why          was    it,        sea,         THAT  YOU   FLED,
4 Tremble,     O      earth,     be -         FORE  THE   LORD,
5 Glory   be   to     the    Father,   and    TO    THE   SON,
```

```
1 Jacob's      sons    from     an           A - LIEN PEOPLE,
2 the          Jordan  turned   back         ON    ITS   COURSE,
3 that    you  turned  back,    Jordan,      ON    YOUR  COURSE?
4 in      the  presence  of     the          GOD   OF    JACOB,
5 and          to       the                  HO -  LY    SPIRIT,
```

```
1 Judah               became               THE . LORD'S TEMPLE,
2 the                 mountains             LEAPT LIKE    RAMS
3 Mountains,     that          you          LEAPT LIKE    RAMS,
4 who      turns  the   rock   in -         TO    A       POOL
5 as  it   was in  the  beginning,  is  now, and  E - VER SHALL BE,
```

```
1 Israel              be        -           CAME  HIS   KINGDOM.
2 and     the   hills         like          YEAR - LING SHEEP.
3 hills,        like                        YEAR - LING SHEEP?
4 and     flint into          a             SPRING OF   WATER.
5 world         without                     END.  A -   MEN.
```

Psalm 113a

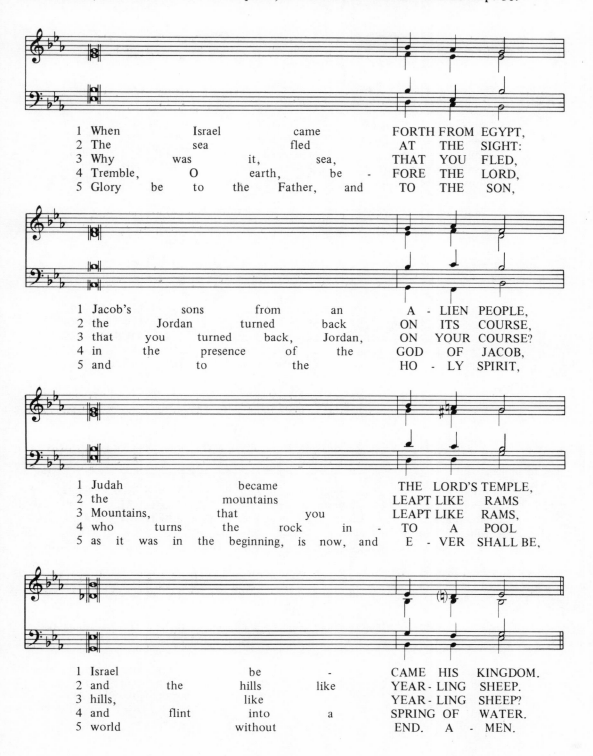

ANTIPHON (recited before and after the psalm). A selection of texts will be found on p. 50.

1 When Israel came FORTH FROM EGYPT,
2 The sea fled AT THE SIGHT:
3 Why was it, sea, THAT YOU FLED,
4 Tremble, O earth, be - FORE THE LORD,
5 Glory be to the Father, and TO THE SON,

1 Jacob's sons from an A - LIEN PEOPLE,
2 the Jordan turned back ON ITS COURSE,
3 that you turned back, Jordan, ON YOUR COURSE?
4 in the presence of the GOD OF JACOB,
5 and to the HO - LY SPIRIT,

1 Judah became THE LORD'S TEMPLE,
2 the mountains LEAPT LIKE RAMS
3 Mountains, that you LEAPT LIKE RAMS,
4 who turns the rock in - TO A POOL
5 as it was in the beginning, is now, and E - VER SHALL BE,

1 Israel be - CAME HIS KINGDOM.
2 and the hills like YEAR - LING SHEEP.
3 hills, like YEAR - LING SHEEP?
4 and flint into a SPRING OF WATER.
5 world without END. A - MEN.

10

Psalm 113a

ANTIPHON (recited before and after the psalm). A selection of texts will be found on p. 50.

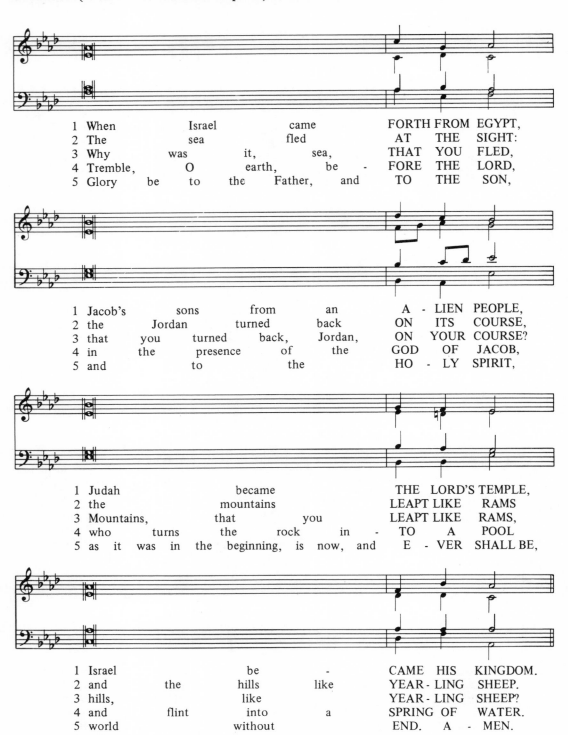

1 When Israel came FORTH FROM EGYPT,
2 The sea fled AT THE SIGHT:
3 Why was it, sea, THAT YOU FLED,
4 Tremble, O earth, be - FORE THE LORD,
5 Glory be to the Father, and TO THE SON,

1 Jacob's sons from an A - LIEN PEOPLE,
2 the Jordan turned back ON ITS COURSE,
3 that you turned back, Jordan, ON YOUR COURSE?
4 in the presence of the GOD OF JACOB,
5 and to the HO - LY SPIRIT,

1 Judah became THE LORD'S TEMPLE,
2 the mountains LEAPT LIKE RAMS
3 Mountains, that you LEAPT LIKE RAMS,
4 who turns the rock in - TO A POOL
5 as it was in the beginning, is now, and E - VER SHALL BE,

1 Israel be - CAME HIS KINGDOM.
2 and the hills like YEAR - LING SHEEP.
3 hills, like YEAR - LING SHEEP?
4 and flint into a SPRING OF WATER.
5 world without END. A - MEN.

Psalm 113a

11

ANTIPHON (recited before and after the psalm). A selection of texts will be found on p. 50.

1 When   Israel   came   FORTH FROM EGYPT,
2 The   sea   fled   AT   THE   SIGHT:
3 Why   was   it,   sea,   THAT YOU   FLED,
4 Tremble,   O   earth,   be -   FORE   THE   LORD,
5 Glory   be   to   the   Father,   and   TO   THE   SON,

1 Jacob's   sons   from   an   A - LIEN PEOPLE,
2 the   Jordan   turned   back   ON   ITS   COURSE,
3 that   you   turned   back,   Jordan,   ON YOUR COURSE?
4 in   the   presence   of   the   GOD   OF   JACOB,
5 and   to   the   HO - LY   SPIRIT,

1 Judah   became   THE   LORD'S TEMPLE,
2 the   mountains   LEAPT LIKE   RAMS
3 Mountains,   that   you   LEAPT LIKE   RAMS,
4 who   turns   the   rock   in -   TO   A   POOL
5 as it was in the beginning, is now, and   E - VER SHALL BE,

1 Israel   be   -   CAME HIS   KINGDOM.
2 and   the   hills   like   YEAR - LING   SHEEP.
3 hills,   like   YEAR - LING   SHEEP?
4 and   flint   into   a   SPRING OF   WATER.
5 world   without   END.   A -   MEN.

12 Psalm 113a

ANTIPHON (recited before and after the psalm). A selection of texts will be found on p. 50.

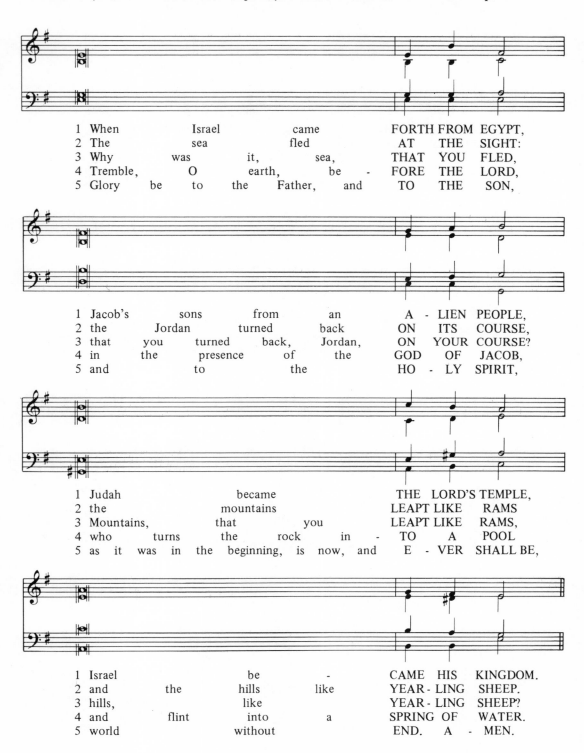

1 When Israel came FORTH FROM EGYPT,
2 The sea fled AT THE SIGHT:
3 Why was it, sea, THAT YOU FLED,
4 Tremble, O earth, be - FORE THE LORD,
5 Glory be to the Father, and TO THE SON,

1 Jacob's sons from an A - LIEN PEOPLE,
2 the Jordan turned back ON ITS COURSE,
3 that you turned back, Jordan, ON YOUR COURSE?
4 in the presence of the GOD OF JACOB,
5 and to the HO - LY SPIRIT,

1 Judah became THE LORD'S TEMPLE,
2 the mountains LEAPT LIKE RAMS
3 Mountains, that you LEAPT LIKE RAMS,
4 who turns the rock in - TO A POOL
5 as it was in the beginning, is now, and E - VER SHALL BE,

1 Israel be - CAME HIS KINGDOM.
2 and the hills like YEAR - LING SHEEP.
3 hills, like YEAR - LING SHEEP?
4 and flint into a SPRING OF WATER.
5 world without END. A - MEN.

Psalm 113a

ANTIPHON (recited before and after the psalm). A selection of texts will be found on p. 50.

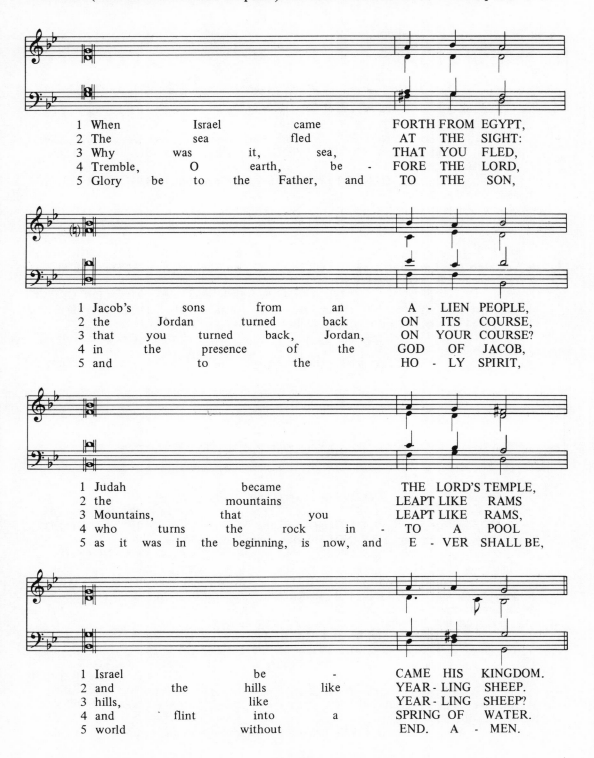

1 When Israel came FORTH FROM EGYPT,
2 The sea fled AT THE SIGHT:
3 Why was it, sea, THAT YOU FLED,
4 Tremble, O earth, be - FORE THE LORD,
5 Glory be to the Father, and TO THE SON,

1 Jacob's sons from an A - LIEN PEOPLE,
2 the Jordan turned back ON ITS COURSE,
3 that you turned back, Jordan, ON YOUR COURSE?
4 in the presence of the GOD OF JACOB,
5 and to the HO - LY SPIRIT,

1 Judah became THE LORD'S TEMPLE,
2 the mountains LEAPT LIKE RAMS
3 Mountains, that you LEAPT LIKE RAMS,
4 who turns the rock in - TO A POOL
5 as it was in the beginning, is now, and E - VER SHALL BE,

1 Israel be - CAME HIS KINGDOM.
2 and the hills like YEAR - LING SHEEP.
3 hills, like YEAR - LING SHEEP?
4 and flint into a SPRING OF WATER.
5 world without END. A - MEN.

14   Psalm 113b

ANTIPHON (recited before and after the psalm). A selection of texts will be found on p. 50.

1 Not to us, Lord, NOT TO US,   but to your name GIVE THE GLORY
2 But our God is   IN THE HEAVENS; he does what - EVER HE WILLS.
3 They have mouths
     but they CAN-NOT SPEAK; they have eyes but they CAN-NOT SEE;
4 With their hands they
     cannot feel; with their
       feet they CAN -NOT WALK. No sound comes FROM THEIR
                                      THROATS.
5 Sons of Israel, trust   IN THE LORD;   he is their help AND THEIR SHIELD.
6 You who fear him, trust IN THE LORD: he is their help AND THEIR SHIELD.
7 The Lord will bless THOSE WHO
               FEAR HIM, the little no less THAN THE GREAT:
8 May you be blessed BY THE LORD, the maker of   HEAVEN AND EARTH.
9 The dead shall not PRAISE THE LORD, nor those who go
                             down INTO THE SILENCE.
10 Glory be to the Father,
           and TO THE SON,   and to the   HO - LY SPIRIT,

1 for the sake of your
         love AND YOUR TRUTH, lest the heathen say:
                            'Where IS THEIR GOD?'
2 Their idols are sil - VER AND GOLD, the work of   HU -MAN HANDS.
3 they have ears but they CAN -NOT HEAR; they have nostrils
                          but they CAN-NOT SMELL.
4 Their makers will
         come to   BE LIKE THEM and so will all who TRUST IN THEM.
5 Sons of Aaron, trust   IN THE LORD; he is their help AND THEIR SHIELD.
6 He remembers us and he
     will bless us;† he will
         bless the SONS OF ISRAEL. He will bless the   SONS OF AARON.
7 To you may the LORD GRANT
                 INCREASE, to you and   ALL YOUR
                                   CHILDREN.
8 The heavens belong TO THE LORD but the earth he has GIVEN TO MEN.
9 But we who live BLESS THE LORD now and for e - VER A -MEN.
10 as it was in the beginning,
         is now, and E - VER SHALL BE, world without END. A -MEN.

16

Psalm 113b

ANTIPHON (recited before and after the psalm). A selection of texts will be found on p. 50.

1 Not to us, Lord, NOT TO US, but to your name GIVE THE GLORY
2 But our God is IN THE HEAVENS; he does what - EVER HE WILLS.
3 They have mouths
    but they CAN-NOT SPEAK; they have eyes but they CAN-NOT SEE;
4 With their hands they
    cannot feel; with their
        feet they CAN-NOT WALK. No sound comes FROM THEIR
                                                THROATS.
5 Sons of Israel, trust IN THE LORD; he is their help AND THEIR SHIELD.
6 You who fear him, trust IN THE LORD: he is their help AND THEIR SHIELD.
7 The Lord will bless THOSE WHO
        FEAR HIM, the little no less THAN THE GREAT:
8 May you be blessed BY THE LORD, the maker of HEAVEN AND EARTH.
9 The dead shall not PRAISE THE LORD, nor those who go
                                        down INTO THE SILENCE.
10 Glory be to the Father,
        and TO THE SON, and to the HO - LY SPIRIT,

1 for the sake of your
    love AND YOUR TRUTH, lest the heathen say:
                                'Where IS THEIR GOD?'
2 Their idols are sil - VER AND GOLD, the work of HU -MAN HANDS.
3 they have ears but they CAN-NOT HEAR; they have nostrils
                                but they CAN-NOT SMELL.
4 Their makers will
        come to BE LIKE THEM and so will all who TRUST IN THEM.
5 Sons of Aaron, trust IN THE LORD; he is their help AND THEIR SHIELD.
6 He remembers us and he
    will bless us;† he will
        bless the SONS OF ISRAEL. He will bless the SONS OF AARON.
7 To you may the LORD GRANT
        INCREASE, to you and ALL YOUR
                                CHILDREN.
8 The heavens belong TO THE LORD but the earth he has GIVEN TO MEN.
9 But we who live BLESS THE LORD now and for e - VER A -MEN.
10 as it was in the beginning,
        is now, and E - VER SHALL BE, world without END. A -MEN.

ANTIPHON (recited before and after the psalm). A selection of texts will be found on p. 50.

1 Not to us, Lord, NOT TO US, but to your name GIVE THE GLORY
2 But our God is IN THE HEAVENS; he does what - EVER HE WILLS.
3 They have mouths
but they CAN-NOT SPEAK; they have eyes but they CAN-NOT SEE;
4 With their hands they
cannot feel; with their
feet they CAN-NOT WALK. No sound comes FROM THEIR
THROATS.
5 Sons of Israel, trust IN THE LORD; he is their help AND THEIR SHIELD.
6 You who fear him, trust IN THE LORD: he is their help AND THEIR SHIELD.
7 The Lord will bless THOSE WHO
FEAR HIM, the little no less THAN THE GREAT:
8 May you be blessed BY THE LORD, the maker of HEAVEN AND EARTH.
9 The dead shall not PRAISE THE LORD, nor those who go
down INTO THE SILENCE.
10 Glory be to the Father,
and TO THE SON, and to the HO - LY SPIRIT,

1 for the sake of your
love AND YOUR TRUTH, lest the heathen say:
'Where IS THEIR GOD?'
2 Their idols are sil - VER AND GOLD, the work of HU -MAN HANDS.
3 they have ears but they CAN - NOT HEAR; they have nostrils
but they CAN-NOT SMELL.
4 Their makers will
come to BE LIKE THEM and so will all who TRUST IN THEM.
5 Sons of Aaron, trust IN THE LORD; he is their help AND THEIR SHIELD.
6 He remembers us and he
will bless us;† he will
bless the SONS OF ISRAEL. He will bless the SONS OF AARON.
7 To you may the LORD GRANT
INCREASE, to you and ALL YOUR
CHILDREN.
8 The heavens belong TO THE LORD but the earth he has GIVEN TO MEN.
9 But we who live BLESS THE LORD now and for e - VER A -MEN.
10 as it was in the beginning,
is now, and E - VER SHALL BE, world without END. A -MEN.

Psalm 113b

ANTIPHON (recited before and after the psalm). A selection of texts will be found on p. 50.

1 Not to us, Lord, NOT TO US, but to your name GIVE THE GLORY
2 But our God is IN THE HEAVENS; he does what - EVER HE WILLS.
3 They have mouths
    but they CAN-NOT SPEAK; they have eyes but they CAN-NOT SEE;
4 With their hands they
    cannot feel; with their
    feet they CAN -NOT WALK. No sound comes FROM THEIR THROATS.
5 Sons of Israel, trust IN THE LORD; he is their help AND THEIR SHIELD.
6 You who fear him, trust IN THE LORD: he is their help AND THEIR SHIELD.
7 The Lord will bless THOSE WHO
    FEAR HIM, the little no less THAN THE GREAT:
8 May you be blessed BY THE LORD, the maker of HEAVEN AND EARTH.
9 The dead shall not PRAISE THE LORD, nor those who go
    down INTO THE SILENCE.
10 Glory be to the Father,
    and TO THE SON, and to the HO - LY SPIRIT,

1 for the sake of your
    love AND YOUR TRUTH, lest the heathen say:
    'Where IS THEIR GOD?'
2 Their idols are sil - VER AND GOLD, the work of HU -MAN HANDS.
3 they have ears but they CAN -NOT HEAR; they have nostrils
    but they CAN-NOT SMELL.
4 Their makers will
    come to BE LIKE THEM and so will all who TRUST IN THEM.
5 Sons of Aaron, trust IN THE LORD; he is their help AND THEIR SHIELD.
6 He remembers us and he
    will bless us;† he will
    bless the SONS OF ISRAEL. He will bless the SONS OF AARON.
7 To you may the LORD GRANT
    INCREASE, to you and ALL YOUR CHILDREN.
8 The heavens belong TO THE LORD but the earth he has GIVEN TO MEN.
9 But we who live BLESS THE LORD now and for e - VER A -MEN.
10 as it was in the beginning,
    is now, and E - VER SHALL BE, world without END. A -MEN.

18

Psalm 113b

ANTIPHON (recited before and after the psalm). A selection of texts will be found on p. 50.

1 Not to us, Lord, NOT TO US, but to your name GIVE THE GLORY
2 But our God is IN THE HEAVENS; he does what - EVER HE WILLS.
3 They have mouths
but they CAN-NOT SPEAK; they have eyes but they CAN-NOT SEE;
4 With their hands they
cannot feel; with their
feet they CAN -NOT WALK. No sound comes FROM THEIR
THROATS.
5 Sons of Israel, trust IN THE LORD; he is their help AND THEIR SHIELD.
6 You who fear him, trust IN THE LORD: he is their help AND THEIR SHIELD.
7 The Lord will bless THOSE WHO
FEAR HIM, the little no less THAN THE GREAT:
8 May you be blessed BY THE LORD, the maker of HEAVEN AND EARTH.
9 The dead shall not PRAISE THE LORD, nor those who go
down INTO THE SILENCE.
10 Glory be to the Father,
and TO THE SON, and to the HO - LY SPIRIT,

1 for the sake of your
love AND YOUR TRUTH, lest the heathen say:
'Where IS THEIR GOD?'
2 Their idols are sil - VER AND GOLD, the work of HU -MAN HANDS.
3 they have ears but they CAN -NOT HEAR; they have nostrils
but they CAN-NOT SMELL.
4 Their makers will
come to BE LIKE THEM and so will all who TRUST IN THEM.
5 Sons of Aaron, trust IN THE LORD; he is their help AND THEIR SHIELD.
6 He remembers us and he
will bless us;† he will
bless the SONS OF ISRAEL. He will bless the SONS OF AARON.
7 To you may the LORD GRANT
INCREASE, to you and ALL YOUR
CHILDREN.
8 The heavens belong TO THE LORD but the earth he has GIVEN TO MEN.
9 But we who live BLESS THE LORD now and for e - VER A -MEN.
10 as it was in the beginning,
is now, and E - VER SHALL BE, world without END. A -MEN.

Psalm 110

ANTIPHON (recited before and after the psalm). A selection of texts will be found on p. 50.

1 I will thank the Lord
  with   ALL MY HEART   in the meeting of the
                            just   and   THEIR AS-SEMBLY.

2 Majestic and glo - RIOUS HIS WORK, his justice stands FIRM FOR EVER.

3 He gives food to THOSE WHO
                     FEAR HIM; keeps his covenant EVER IN MIND.

4 His works are jus - TICE AND TRUTH: his precepts are all OF THEM SURE,

5 He has sent deliverance
  to his people† and
  established his cove - NANT FOR EVER. Holy his name, TO BE FEARED.

6 Glory be to the
  Father   and   TO THE SON, and to the HO - LY SPIRIT,

1 Great are the works OF THE LORD; to be pondered by ALL WHO
                                                      LOVE THEM.

2 He makes us remem - BER HIS WONDERS. The Lord is compas - SION AND LOVE.

3 He has shown his might TO HIS PEOPLE by giving them the
                                     lands   OF THE NATIONS.

4 standing firm for e - VER AND EVER: they are made in
                                     upright   -   NESS AND TRUTH.

5 To fear the Lord is the
  first stage of wisdom;†
  all who do so prove THEM-SELVES WISE. His praise shall LAST FOR EVER.

6 as it was in the beginning,
  is   now,   and   E - VER SHALL BE, world   without   END. A - MEN.

ANTIPHON (recited before and after the psalm). A selection of texts will be found on p. 50.

1 I will thank the Lord
  with   ALL MY HEART   in the meeting of the
                           just   and   THEIR AS-SEMBLY.

2 Majestic   and   glo - RIOUS HIS WORK,   his justice stands FIRM FOR EVER.

3 He gives food to THOSE WHO
                        FEAR HIM; keeps his covenant   EVER IN MIND.

4 His works are jus - TICE AND TRUTH: his precepts are all   OF THEM SURE,

5 He has sent deliverance
  to his people† and
  established his cove- NANT FOR EVER.   Holy   his   name,   TO BE FEARED.

6 Glory be to the
  Father   and   TO THE SON,   and   to   the   HO - LY SPIRIT,

1 Great are the works OF THE LORD;   to be pondered by ALL WHO
                                                              LOVE THEM.

2 He makes us remem - BER HIS WONDERS. The Lord is compas - SION AND LOVE.

3 He has shown his might TO HIS PEOPLE   by giving them the
                                     lands   OF THE NATIONS.

4 standing firm for e - VER AND EVER: they are made in
                                    upright   -   NESS AND TRUTH.

5 To fear the Lord is the
  first stage of wisdom;†
  all who do so prove THEM-SELVES WISE. His praise shall   LAST FOR EVER.

6 as it was in the beginning,
  is   now,   and   E - VER SHALL BE, world   without   END. A - MEN.

Psalm 110

ANTIPHON (recited before and after the psalm). A selection of texts will be found on p. 50.

1 I will thank the Lord
with ALL MY HEART in the meeting of the
just and THEIR AS-SEMBLY.

2 Majestic and glo - RIOUS HIS WORK, his justice stands FIRM FOR EVER.

3 He gives food to THOSE WHO
FEAR HIM; keeps his covenant EVER IN MIND.

4 His works are jus - TICE AND TRUTH: his precepts are all OF THEM SURE,

5 He has sent deliverance
to his people† and
established his cove - NANT FOR EVER. Holy his name, TO BE FEARED.

6 Glory be to the
Father and TO THE SON, and to the HO - LY SPIRIT,

1 Great are the works OF THE LORD; to be pondered by ALL WHO
LOVE THEM.

2 He makes us remem - BER HIS WONDERS. The Lord is compas - SION AND LOVE.

3 He has shown his might TO HIS PEOPLE by giving them the
lands OF THE NATIONS.

4 standing firm for e - VER AND EVER: they are made in
upright - NESS AND TRUTH.

5 To fear the Lord is the
first stage of wisdom;†
all who do so prove THEM-SELVES WISE. His praise shall LAST FOR EVER.

6 as it was in the beginning,
is now, and E - VER SHALL BE, world without END. A - MEN.

ANTIPHON (recited before and after the psalm). A selection of texts will be found on p. 50.

1 I will thank the Lord
   with ALL MY HEART in the meeting of the
   just and THEIR AS-SEMBLY.

2 Majestic and glo - RIOUS HIS WORK, his justice stands FIRM FOR EVER.

3 He gives food to THOSE WHO
   FEAR HIM; keeps his covenant EVER IN MIND.

4 His works are jus - TICE AND TRUTH: his precepts are all OF THEM SURE,

5 He has sent deliverance
   to his people† and
   established his cove - NANT FOR EVER. Holy his name, TO BE FEARED.

6 Glory be to the
   Father and TO THE SON, and to the HO - LY SPIRIT,

1 Great are the works OF THE LORD; to be pondered by ALL WHO
   LOVE THEM.

2 He makes us remem - BER HIS WONDERS. The Lord is compas - SION AND LOVE.

3 He has shown his might TO HIS PEOPLE by giving them the
   lands OF THE NATIONS.

4 standing firm for e - VER AND EVER: they are made in
   upright - NESS AND TRUTH.

5 To fear the Lord is the
   first stage of wisdom;†
   all who do so prove THEM-SELVES WISE. His praise shall LAST FOR EVER.

6 as it was in the beginning,
   is now, and E - VER SHALL BE, world without END. A - MEN.

Psalm 110

ANTIPHON (recited before and after the psalm). A selection of texts will be found on p. 50.

1 I will thank the Lord
with ALL MY HEART in the meeting of the
just and THEIR AS-SEMBLY.

2 Majestic and glo - RIOUS HIS WORK, his justice stands FIRM FOR EVER.

3 He gives food to THOSE WHO
FEAR HIM; keeps his covenant EVER IN MIND.

4 His works are jus - TICE AND TRUTH: his precepts are all OF THEM SURE,

5 He has sent deliverance
to his people† and
established his cove - NANT FOR EVER. Holy his name, TO BE FEARED.

6 Glory be to the
Father and TO THE SON, and to the HO - LY SPIRIT,

1 Great are the works OF THE LORD; to be pondered by ALL WHO
LOVE THEM.

2 He makes us remem - BER HIS WONDERS. The Lord is compas - SION AND LOVE.

3 He has shown his might TO HIS PEOPLE by giving them the
lands OF THE NATIONS.

4 standing firm for e - VER AND EVER: they are made in
upright - NESS AND TRUTH.

5 To fear the Lord is the
first stage of wisdom;†
all who do so prove THEM-SELVES WISE. His praise shall LAST FOR EVER.

6 as it was in the beginning,
is now, and E - VER SHALL BE, world without END. A - MEN.

24　　Psalm 110

ANTIPHON (recited before and after the psalm). A selection of texts will be found on p. 50.

1　I will thank the Lord
　with　　　　　　　　ALL MY HEART　　in the meeting of the
　　　　　　　　　　　　　　　　　　just　　and　　THEIR AS-SEMBLY.

2　Majestic　and　glo - RIOUS HIS WORK,　his　justice　stands　FIRM FOR EVER.

3　He　gives　food　to　THOSE WHO
　　　　　　　　　　　　FEAR HIM;　keeps his covenant　EVER IN MIND.

4　His　works　are　jus - TICE AND TRUTH:　his　precepts　are all　OF THEM SURE,

5　He has sent deliverance
　to his people† and
　established his cove - NANT FOR EVER.　Holy　his　name,　TO BE FEARED.

6　Glory be to the
　Father　　and　　TO THE SON,　and　　to　　the　　HO - LY SPIRIT,

1　Great　are　the　works　OF THE LORD;　to　be　pondered by　ALL WHO
　　　　　　　　　　　　　　　　　　　　　　　　　　　　　LOVE THEM.

2　He　makes　us　remem - BER HIS WONDERS. The　Lord　is compas - SION AND LOVE.

3　He has shown his might　TO HIS PEOPLE　by giving them the
　　　　　　　　　　　　　　　　　lands　　　　　　OF THE NATIONS.

4　standing　firm　for e - VER AND EVER:　they　are　made in
　　　　　　　　　　　　　　　　　upright　　-　　NESS AND TRUTH.

5　To fear the Lord is the
　first stage of wisdom;†
　all who do so prove　THEM-SELVES WISE. His　praise　shall　LAST FOR EVER.

6　as it was in the beginning,
　is　　now,　　and　　E - VER SHALL BE, world　　without　　END. A - MEN.

Psalm 111

ANTIPHON (recited before and after the psalm). A selection of texts will be found on p. 50.

1 Happy the man who FEARS THE LORD, who takes delight in all HIS COM-MANDS.
2 Riches and wealth are IN HIS HOUSE; his justice stands FIRM FOR EVER.
3 The good man takes pi - TY AND LENDS. he conducts his af - FAIRS WITH HONOUR.
4 He has no fear of E - VIL NEWS; with a firm heart he
    trusts IN THE LORD.

5 Open-handed, he gives to
   the poor;† his justice
   stands FIRM FOR EVER. His head will be RAISED IN GLORY.
6 Glory be to the Father,
   and TO THE SON, and to the HO - LY SPIRIT,

1 His sons will be power - FUL ON EARTH; the children of the up -RIGHT ARE
    BLESSED.

2 He is a light in the
   darkness FOR THE UPRIGHT: he is generous, merci- FUL AND JUST.
3 The just man will NE - VER WAVER: he will be remem - BERED FOR EVER.
4 With a steadfast heart he WILL NOT FEAR; he will see the downfall OF HIS FOES.
5 The wicked man sees and
   is angry,† grinds his
   teeth and FADES A - WAY; the desire of the wicked LEADS TO DOOM.
6 as it was in the
   beginning, is now, and E - VER
    SHALL BE, world without END. A -MEN.

ANTIPHON (recited before and after the psalm). A selection of texts will be found on p. 50.

1 Happy the man who FEARS THE LORD,   who takes delight in all HIS COM-MANDS.
2 Riches and wealth are   IN HIS HOUSE;   his justice stands   FIRM FOR EVER.
3 The good man takes pi - TY AND LENDS,   he conducts his af - FAIRS WITH HONOUR.
4 He has no fear of   E - VIL NEWS;   with a firm heart he
      trusts   IN THE LORD.

5 Open-handed, he gives to
   the poor;† his justice
   stands   FIRM FOR EVER.   His head will be RAISED IN GLORY.
6 Glory be to the Father,
   and   TO THE SON,   and to the   HO - LY SPIRIT,

1 His sons will be power - FUL ON EARTH;   the children of the up -RIGHT ARE
                                           BLESSED.

2 He is a light in the
   darkness   FOR THE UPRIGHT: he is generous, merci- FUL AND JUST.
3 The just man will   NE - VER WAVER: he will be remem - BERED FOR EVER.
4 With a steadfast heart he WILL NOT FEAR;   he will see the downfall OF HIS FOES.
5 The wicked man sees and
   is angry;† grinds his
   teeth   and   FADES A - WAY;   the desire of the wicked LEADS TO DOOM.
6 as it was in the
   beginning, is now, and   E - VER
                SHALL BE, world   without   END. A - MEN.

Psalm 111

ANTIPHON (recited before and after the psalm). A selection of texts will be found on p. 50.

1 Happy the man who FEARS THE LORD,   who takes delight in all HIS COM-MANDS.
2 Riches and wealth are IN HIS HOUSE;   his justice stands FIRM FOR EVER.
3 The good man takes pi - TY AND LENDS,   he conducts his af - FAIRS WITH HONOUR
4 He has no fear of E - VIL NEWS;   with a firm heart he
     trusts   IN THE LORD.

5 Open-handed, he gives to
   the poor;† his justice
   stands   FIRM FOR EVER.   His head will be RAISED IN GLORY.
6 Glory be to the Father,
   and   TO THE SON,   and to the HO - LY SPIRIT,

1 His sons will be power - FUL ON EARTH;   the children of the up -RIGHT ARE
     BLESSED.

2 He is a light in the
   darkness   FOR THE UPRIGHT: he is generous, merci- FUL AND JUST.
3 The just man will NE - VER WAVER: he will be remem - BERED FOR EVER.
4 With a steadfast heart he WILL NOT FEAR; he will see the downfall OF HIS FOES.
5 The wicked man sees and
   is angry;† grinds his
   teeth and FADES A - WAY;   the desire of the wicked LEADS TO DOOM.
6 as it was in the
   beginning, is now, and E - VER
     SHALL BE, world without END. A - MEN.

Psalm 111

ANTIPHON (recited before and after the psalm). A selection of texts will be found on p. 50.

1 Happy the man who FEARS THE LORD, who takes delight in all HIS COM-MANDS.
2 Riches and wealth are IN HIS HOUSE; his justice stands FIRM FOR EVER.
3 The good man takes pi - TY AND LENDS, he conducts his af - FAIRS WITH HONOUR.
4 He has no fear of E - VIL NEWS; with a firm heart he
  trusts IN THE LORD.

5 Open-handed, he gives to
  the poor;† his justice
  stands FIRM FOR EVER. His head will be RAISED IN GLORY.
6 Glory be to the Father,
  and TO THE SON, and to the HO - LY SPIRIT,

1 His sons will be power -FUL ON EARTH; the children of the up -RIGHT ARE
  BLESSED.

2 He is a light in the
  darkness FOR THE UPRIGHT: he is generous, merci-FUL AND JUST.
3 The just man will NE - VER WAVER: he will be remem - BERED FOR EVER.
4 With a steadfast heart he WILL NOT FEAR; he will see the downfall OF HIS FOES.
5 The wicked man sees and
  is angry;† grinds his
  teeth and FADES A - WAY; the desire of the wicked LEADS TO DOOM.
6 as it was in the
  beginning, is now, and E - VER
  SHALL BE, world without END. A - MEN.

Psalm 111

ANTIPHON (recited before and after the psalm). A selection of texts will be found on p. 50.

1 Happy the man who FEARS THE LORD, who takes delight in all HIS COM-MANDS.
2 Riches and wealth are IN HIS HOUSE; his justice stands FIRM FOR EVER.
3 The good man takes pi- TY AND LENDS, he conducts his af - FAIRS WITH HONOUR.
4 He has no fear of E - VIL NEWS; with a firm heart he
trusts IN THE LORD.

5 Open-handed, he gives to
the poor;† his justice
stands FIRM FOR EVER. His head will be RAISED IN GLORY.
6 Glory be to the Father,
and TO THE SON, and to the HO - LY SPIRIT,

1 His sons will be power -FUL ON EARTH; the children of the up -RIGHT ARE
BLESSED.

2 He is a light in the
darkness FOR THE UPRIGHT: he is generous, merci- FUL AND JUST.
3 The just man will NE - VER WAVER: he will be remem - BERED FOR EVER.
4 With a steadfast heart he WILL NOT FEAR; he will see the downfall OF HIS FOES.
5 The wicked man sees and
is angry;† grinds his
teeth and FADES A - WAY; the desire of the wicked LEADS TO DOOM.
6 as it was in the
beginning, is now, and E - VER
SHALL BE, world without END. A -MEN.

ANTIPHON (recited before and after the psalm). A selection of texts will be found on p. 50.

1 Happy the man who FEARS THE LORD, who takes delight in all HIS COM-MANDS.
2 Riches and wealth are IN HIS HOUSE; his justice stands FIRM FOR EVER.
3 The good man takes pi - TY AND LENDS, he conducts his af - FAIRS WITH HONOUR.
4 He has no fear of E - VIL NEWS; with a firm heart he
  trusts IN THE LORD.

5 Open-handed, he gives to
  the poor;† his justice
  stands FIRM FOR EVER. His head will be RAISED IN GLORY.
6 Glory be to the Father,
  and TO THE SON, and to the HO - LY SPIRIT,

1 His sons will be power -FUL ON EARTH; the children of the up -RIGHT ARE
  BLESSED.

2 He is a light in the
  darkness FOR THE UPRIGHT: he is generous, merci- FUL AND JUST.
3 The just man will NE - VER WAVER: he will be remem - BERED FOR EVER.
4 With a steadfast heart he WILL NOT FEAR; he will see the downfall OF HIS FOES.
5 The wicked man sees and
  is angry;† grinds his
  teeth and FADES A - WAY; the desire of the wicked LEADS TO DOOM.
6 as it was in the
  beginning, is now, and E - VER
  SHALL BE, world without END. A - MEN.

Canticle

Rev 19: 1, 2, 5-7

ANTIPHON (recited before and after the canticle). A selection of texts will be found on p. 51.

RESPONSE

Al - le - lu - ia, Al - le - lu - ia.

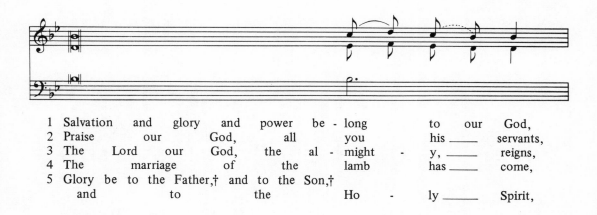

1 Salvation and glory and power be - long to our God,
2 Praise our God, all you his ____ servants,
3 The Lord our God, the al - might - y, ____ reigns,
4 The marriage of the lamb has ____ come,
5 Glory be to the Father,† and to the Son,†
  and to the Ho - ly ____ Spirit,

1 His judge-ments are true and just. ℟
2 You who fear him, small and great. ℟
3 Let us rejoice and exult and give him the glory. ℟
4 And his bride has made her - self ready. ℟
5 As it was in the beginning, is now,
  and ever shall be, world without end. A - men. ℟

32 Canticle

Rev 19: 1, 2, 5-7

ANTIPHON (recited before and after the canticle). A selection of texts will be found on p. 51.

start by singing Alleluia at*

1 Salvation and glory and power
   belong   to our   God,   AL-LE-LU - IA, AL-LE-LU - IA.
2 Praise   our   God,   all   you his   servants, AL-LE-LU - IA, AL-LE-LU - IA.
3 The Lord our God, the Al-might-y,   reigns,   AL-LE-LU - IA, AL-LE-LU - IA.
4 The   marriage   of   the   Lamb has   come,   AL-LE-LU - IA, AL-LE-LU - IA.
5 Glory be to the Father, and to
   the   Son,   and   to   the   Ho - ly   Spirit,   AL-LE-LU - IA, AL-LE-LU - IA.

1 His   judgements   are   true and just.   AL-LE-LU -IA, AL-LE-LU - IA, AL-LE-LU-IA.
2 You   who   fear   him,   small and great   AL-LE-LU -IA, AL-LE-LU - IA, AL-LE-LU-IA.
3 Let us rejoice and exult
   and   give   him the glory   AL-LE-LU -IA, AL-LE-LU - IA, AL-LE-LU-IA.
4 And his bride has made her - self ready.   AL-LE-LU -IA, AL-LE-LU - IA, AL-LE-LU-IA.
5 As it was in the beginning,
   is now and ever shall be,
   world   without   end. A - men.   AL-LE-LU -IA, AL-LE-LU - IA, AL-LE-LU-IA.

Canticle

Rev 19: 1, 2, 5-7

33

ANTIPHON (recited before and after the canticle). A selection of texts will be found on p. 51.

1 Salvation and glory and power be - long to our God.
2 Praise our God all you ___ his servants.
3 The Lord our God, the Al - might - y, reigns.
4 The marriage of the Lamb ___ has come.
5 Praise the Father, the Son and Ho - ly Spirit.

℞ Al - le - lu - ia! 1 His judgements are true ___
℞ Al - le - lu - ia! 2 You who fear him, small ___
℞ Al - le - lu - ia! 3 Let us rejoice and exult and give ___
℞ Al - le - lu - ia! 4 and his bride has made her
℞ Al - le - lu - ia! 5 now and for e -

1 and ___ just. ℞ Al - le - lu - ia, Al - le - lu - ia!
2 and ___ great. ℞ Al - le - lu - ia, Al - le - lu - ia!
3 him the glory. ℞ Al - le - lu - ia, Al - le - lu - ia!
4 -self ___ ready. ℞ Al - le - lu - ia, Al - le - lu - ia!
5 -ver a - men. ℞ Al - le - lu - ia, Al - le - lu - ia!

34 Lenten Canticle
1 Peter 2: 21-24

ANTIPHON (recited before and after the canticle). A selection of texts will be found on p. 51.

℞ BY HIS WOUNDS YOU HAVE BEEN HEALED.

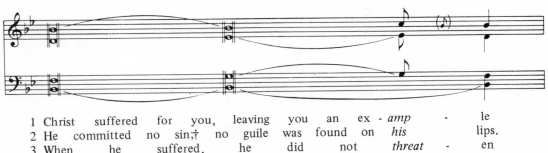

1 Christ suffered for you, leaving you an ex - *amp* - le
2 He committed no sin;† no guile was found on *his* lips.
3 When he suffered, he did not *threat* - en
4 He himself bore our sins in his body *on* the tree,
5 Glory be to the Father, and to the Son, and to the Holy *Spi* - rit,

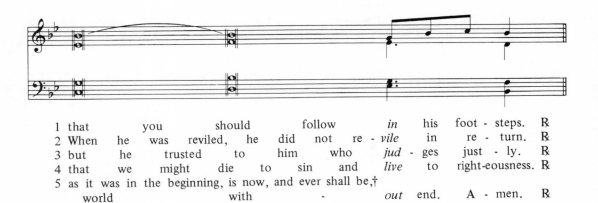

1 that you should follow *in* his foot - steps. ℞
2 When he was reviled, he did not re - *vile* in re - turn. ℞
3 but he trusted to him who *jud* - ges just - ly. ℞
4 that we might die to sin and *live* to right-eousness. ℞
5 as it was in the beginning, is now, and ever shall be,†
    world with - *out* end. A - men. ℞

Easter Canticle

Rev 19: 1, 2, 5-7

35

ANTIPHON (recited before and after the canticle). A selection of texts will be found on p. 51.

RESPONSE

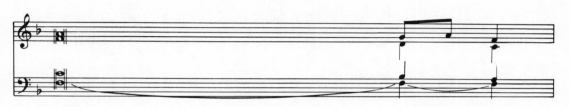

1 Salvation and glory and power be - long to our God.
2 Praise our God all you his servants,
3 The Lord our God, the Al - might - y, reigns;
4 The marriage of the Lamb has come
5 Glory be to the Father, and to the Son, and to the Ho - ly Spirit,

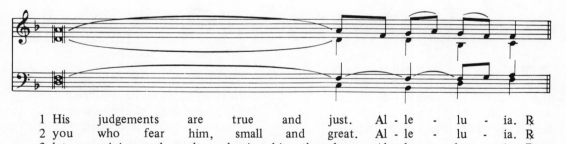

1 His judgements are true and just. Al - le - lu - ia. ℟
2 you who fear him, small and great. Al - le - lu - ia. ℟
3 let us rejoice and exult and give him the glory. Al - le - lu - ia. ℟
4 and his bride has made herself ready. Al - le - lu - ia.
5 as it was in the beginning, is now, and ever ℟
     shall be, world without end. Amen. Al - le - lu - ia. ℟

The Word of God

A reading from scripture, followed by a time of silent reflection and prayer.
THE SHORT RESPONSORY follows. This changes week by week. One example is given:
PLEASE STAND

Cantor:	Great is our Lord; great is his might.
All:	Great is our Lord; great is his might;
Cantor:	His wisdom can never be measured.
All:	Great is our Lord; great is his might.
Cantor:	Glory be to the Father, and to the Son, and to the Holy Spirit.
All:	Great is our Lord; great is his might.

It may be helpful to sing one of the following verses (37-47):

37

Blessed Jesus, at your word
we are gathered all to hear you;
let our hearts and minds be stirred
now to seek and love and fear you;
by your teachings true and holy
drawn from earth to love you solely.

38

Word of God, come down on earth,
living rain from heaven descending;
touch our hearts and bring to birth
faith and hope and love unending.
Word almighty, we revere you;
Word made flesh, we long to hear you.

39

Word that speaks your Father's love,
one with him beyond all telling,
Word that sends us from above
God the Spirit, with us dwelling,
Word of truth, to all truth lead us,
Word of life, with one Bread feed us.

40 Lord, thy word abideth,
and our footsteps guideth;
who its truth believeth
light and joy receiveth.

O that we discerning
its most holy learning,
Lord, may love and fear thee,
evermore be near thee. **41**

42 In the scriptures, by the Spirit,
may we see the Saviour's face,
hear his word and heed his calling,
know his will and grow in grace.

Saviour, give thy living Spirit
to the preaching of thy word,
so that, saved and taught and challenged,
we may teach what we have heard. **43**

44 Speak to us, O Lord, believing,
as we hear, the sower sows;
may our hearts, your word receiving,
be the good ground where it grows.

45 Praise we now the Word of grace;
may our hearts its truth embrace:
from its pages may we hear
Christ our teacher, speaking clear.

May the Gospel of the Lord
everywhere be spread abroad,
that the whole wide world may own
Christ as King, and Christ alone. **46**

47 Your words to me are full of joy,
of beauty, peace and grace;
from them I learn your blessed will,
through them I see your face.

48 The Magnificat

The Canticle of Mary

ANTIPHON (recited before and after the Magnificat): changes every Sunday of the year.
During the Magnificat the Blessed Sacrament, the altar, the ministers and the people are incensed.

1 My soul glori - FIES THE LORD, my spirit rejoices in GOD, my Sav - iour.
2 He looks on his
servant IN HER LOWLINESS; henceforth all ages
will CALL me bless - ed.
3 The Almighty works
marvels for me. HOLY HIS NAME! His mercy is from
age to age, on THOSE who fear him.
4 He puts forth his
arm in strength
and scatters THE PROUD - HEARTED. He casts the mighty
from their thrones
and RAIS -es the lowly.
5 He fills the starving WITH GOOD THINGS, sends the RICH away emp - ty.
6 He protects Israel,
his servant, re - MEMBER-ING
HIS MERCY, the mercy promised
to our Fathers,†
to Abraham and his SONS for ev - er.
7 Glory be to the
Father and to the
Son and to the HO - LY SPIRIT; as it was in the
beginning† is now
and ever shall be† WORLD with-out
end A-men.

The Magnificat

The Canticle of Mary

1 My soul proclaims the Lord my God,
  my spirit sings his praise!
  He looks on me, he lifts me up,
  and gladness fills my days.

2 All nations now will share my joy,
  his gifts he has outpoured;
  his little ones he has made great;
  I magnify the Lord.

3 His mercy is for evermore!
  His name I praise again!
  His strong right arm puts down the proud
  and raises lowly men!

4 He fills the hungry with good things,
  the rich he sends away.
  The promise made to Abraham
  is kept by him each day.

5 All praise to God the Father be,
  all glory to the Son,
  whom with the Spirit we adore:
  our God, for ever one.

49

50 The Magnificat

The Canticle of Mary

1 My soul, give glory to the Lord on high;
   in God my Saviour do I now rejoice.

2 He sees his servant in her lowliness;
   all ages now will call me ever blest.

3 He makes me great by his almighty power;
   I praise and bless and glorify his name.

4 All those who fear the Lord, the living God,
   receive his mercy, now and evermore.

5 His arm is strong, the proud of heart dispersed;
   the mighty fall, and lowly ones are raised.

6 The starving poor are laden with his gifts;
   he sends away the rich in emptiness.

7 Mercy is sure for servant Israel,
   in ages past, both now and evermore.

8 Praise, glory, honour to the Trinity:
   the Father, Son and Spirit ever blest.

The Magnificat

The Canticle of Mary

1 Tell out, my soul, the greatness of the Lord!
Unnumbered blessings, give my spirit voice;
tender to me the promise of his word;
in God my Saviour shall my heart rejoice.

2 Tell out, my soul, the greatness of his name!
Make known his might, the deeds his arm has done;
his mercy sure, from age to age the same;
his holy name – the Lord, the Mighty One.

3 Tell out, my soul, the greatness of his might!
Powers and dominions lay their glory by.
Proud hearts and stubborn wills are put to flight,
the hungry fed, the humble lifted high.

4 Tell out, my soul, the glories of his word!
Firm is his promise, and his mercy sure.
Tell out, my soul, the greatness of the Lord
to children's children and for evermore!

The following doxology may be added:

Give praise to God the Father, Lord above;
give praise to Jesus Christ, his only Son;
give praise to him who binds them both in love:
uniquely threefold but for ever One.

52

The Magnificat

The Canticle of Mary

1 Now— my soul shall mag - ni - fy — the Lord, — my God,

and — my spi - rit thrills with joy — in him — who saves.

From hea-ven's height he ga - zes down — with eyes — of love

on — his ser - vant meek — and low - ly and hum-ble of heart.

2 Age after age all generations will call me blest.
God the mighty one, has done great things for me;
His name is holy; all who fear him will mercy find.
The proud of heart his powerful arm indeed brings low.

3 He dethrones the mighty, but exalts the meek;
Though he feeds the starving poor yet he spurns the rich.
Merciful he helps his servant Israel
As he promised to the sons of Abraham.

4 Glorify the Father high enthroned above;
Glorify the Son, Redeemer blest, the Lord;
Glorify the Spirit, fount of joy and peace;
Through all ages may the God of love be praised.

The Magnificat

The Canticle of Mary

1 My soul now glo - ri - fy ___ the Lord who is ___ my Sa - viour. Re -
2 The world shall call me blest ___ and pon - der on ___ my sto - ry. In
3 For those who are his friends ___ and keep his laws ___ as ho - ly, His
4 But by his power the great, ___ the proud, the self - con - ceit - ed, The
5 He feeds the starv - ing poor, ___ he guards his ho - ly na - tion, Ful -
6 Then glo - ri - fy with me ___ the Lord who is ___ my Sa - viour, One

1 joice, ___ for who am I that God ___ has shown me fa - vour.
2 me ___ is ma - ni - fest God's great - ness and ___ his glo - ry.
3 mer - cy ne - ver ends; and he ___ ex - alts ___ the low - ly.
4 kings ___ who sit in state, are hum - bled and ___ de - feat - ed.
5 fill - ing what he swore long since ___ in re - ve - la - tion.
6 ho - ly Tri - ni - ty, For e - ver and ___ for e - ver.

Intercessions

54

At the end of each Intercession, one of the following formulae may be sung.

CANTOR

In peace let us pray to the Lord

ALL

LORD, IN YOUR MERCY, HEAR OUR PRAYER.

55

CANTOR

From our hearts, we pray:

ALL

LORD, LIS - TEN TO OUR PRAYER.

The Intercessions end with the Our Father. Then follows the Concluding Prayer (Collect).

Tantum Ergo

1 Come, adore this wondrous presence,
  bow to Christ, the source of grace.
  Here is kept the ancient promise
  of God's earthly dwelling-place.
  Sight is blind before God's glory,
  faith alone may see his face.

2 Glory be to God the Father,
  praise to his coequal Son,
  adoration to the Spirit,
  bond of love, in Godhead one.
  Blest be God by all Creation
  joyously while ages run.

56

57

Other Eucharistic Hymns may be used in place of the Tantum ergo.

Celebrant   Let us pray.
Lord Jesus Christ,
you gave us the eucharist
as the memorial of your suffering and death.
May our worship of this sacrament of your body and blood
help us to experience the salvation you won for us
and the peace of the kingdom
where you live with the Father and the Holy Spirit,
one God, for ever and ever.

All   Amen.

Other prayers may be used, as given in the rite, Worship of the Eucharist Outside Mass, no 68.

THE BLESSING

The Blessed Sacrament is then reposed in the tabernacle.

The Divine Praises may now be said (optional)

Hymn
(the last number on the board)

PLEASE STAND

ANTIPHONS FOR PSALM 109

Through the Year

Sunday 1:   The Lord will send his mighty sceptre from Sion,
              and he will rule for ever, alleluia.

Sunday 2:   Christ the Lord is a priest for ever
              according to the order of Melchizedek, alleluia.

Sunday 3:   The Lord's revelation to my Master: 'Sit on my right', alleluia.

Sunday 4:   In holy splendour I begot you before the dawn, alleluia.

Advent

Sunday 1:   Rejoice greatly, daughter of Sion,
              shout with gladness, daughter of Jerusalem, alleluia.

Sunday 2:   Behold, the Lord will come on the clouds of heaven
              with great strength, alleluia.

Sunday 3:   See, the Lord will come.
              He will sit with princes and he will mount the glorious throne.

Sunday 4:   See, how splendid is he who comes to save the peoples.

Lent

Sunday 1:   You must worship the Lord, your God, and serve him alone.

Sunday 2:   The Lord will send forth your sceptre of power
              with the splendour of the saints.

Sunday 3:   Lord, almighty king, deliver us for the sake of your name.
              Give us the grace to return to you.

Sunday 4:   God has appointed him to judge everyone, living and dead.

Sunday 5:   As Moses lifted up the serpent in the desert,
              so the Son of Man must be lifted up.

Palm Sunday: He was wounded and humbled,
              but God has raised him up with his own right hand.

Eastertide

Sundays 2 & 6: He raised Christ from the dead
                and placed him at his own right hand, in heaven, alleluia.

Sundays 3 & 7: When he had made purification for sin,
                he sat at the right hand of the Majesty on high, alleluia.

Sunday 4:   You must look for the things of heaven,
                where Christ is, sitting at God's right hand, alleluia.

Sunday 5:   The Lord has risen and sits at the right hand of God, alleluia.

Proper antiphons for other Sundays will be found in *The Divine Office*.

ANTIPHONS FOR PSALM 113A (Sunday 1 of the cycle)

Through the year: The earth trembled before the Lord.

Advent: Christ our King will come. He is the lamb that John announced.

Lent Sunday 1:   Now is the favourable time; this is the day of salvation.

Lent Sunday 5:   The Lord of hosts protects and rescues; he spares and he saves.

Easter (5):   He has freed us from the power of darkness
and has given us a place in the kingdom of his Son, alleluia.

Proper antiphons for other Sundays will be found in *The Divine Office.*

ANTIPHONS FOR PSALM 113B (Sunday 2 of the cycle)

Through the Year: Our God is in heaven: he has power to do whatever he will, alleluia.

Advent: The Lord will come and will not disappoint us.
Wait for him if he seems to delay, for he will surely come, alleluia.

Lent Sunday 2:   We worship the one God, who made heaven and earth.

Palm Sunday: The blood of Christ purifies us to serve the living God.

Easter (2 & 6):   You have been converted from idolatry to the living God, alleluia.

Proper antiphons for other Sundays will be found in *The Divine Office.*

ANTIPHONS FOR PSALM 110 (Sunday 3 of the cycle)

Through the Year: The Lord is full of merciful love;
he makes us remember his wonders, alleluia.

Advent: The mountains will bring forth joy and the hills justice;
for the Lord, the light of the world, comes in strength.

Lent: We were ransomed with the precious blood of Christ,
the lamb who is without blemish.

Easter (3 & 7):   The Lord has delivered his people, alleluia.

Proper antiphons for other Sundays will be found in *The Divine Office.*

ANTIPHONS FOR PSALM 111 (Sunday 4 of the cycle)

Through the Year: Blessed are they who hunger and thirst for justice,
for they shall have their fill.

Advent: The rugged places shall be made smooth
and the mountain-ranges shall become plains.
Come, Lord, and do not delay, alleluia.

Lent: Happy is the man to whom the Lord shows mercy; he will never waver.

Easter (4):   He has risen as a light in the darkness,
for the upright of heart, alleluia.

Proper antiphons for other Sundays will be found in *The Divine Office.*

ANTIPHONS FOR REVELATION CANTICLE (19:1, 2, 5-7)

Through the Year

Sunday 1:   The Lord is King, our God, the Almighty! alleluia.

Sundays 2 & 4:   Praise God, all you his servants, both great and small, alleluia.

Sunday 3:   The Lord our God almighty is king, alleluia.

Advent

Sunday 1:   Behold I am coming soon to reward every man according to his deeds, says the Lord.

Sunday 2:   The Lord is our judge, the Lord is our King.
He will come and make us whole.

Sunday 3:   Let us live justly and honestly
while we are awaiting, in hope, the coming of the Lord.

Sunday 4:   Great will be his reign and peace will be everlasting, alleluia.

Eastertide

Sundays 2 & 6:   Alleluia, victory and glory and power belong to our God, alleluia.

Sundays 3 & 7:   Alleluia, the Lord our God is king;
let us rejoice and give glory to him, alleluia.

Sunday 4:   Alleluia, victory and glory and power to our God, alleluia.

Sunday 5:   Alleluia, the Lord, our God, is King;
let us rejoice and give glory to him, alleluia.

ANTIPHONS FOR LENTEN CANTICLE (1 Peter 2:21-24)

Sunday 1:   Now we are going up to Jerusalem,
and everything that is written about the Son of Man will come true.

Sunday 2:   God did not spare his own Son but gave him up for us all.

Sunday 3:   Ours were the sufferings he bore, ours the sorrows he carried.

Sunday 4:   God fulfilled what he had foretold in the words of all the prophets:
that Christ would suffer.

Sunday 5:   He was wounded for our faults, he was bruised for our sins.
Through his wounds we are healed.

Palm Sunday: He carried our sins in his own body on the cross,
so that we might die to sin and live for holiness.

A cassette demonstrating the performance of this music is on
sale from:

Michael Beattie S J,
Sacred Heart Presbytery,
Edge Hill, London SW19 4LU.

Collins Liturgical Publications
187 Piccadilly, London W1V 9DA

Collins Liturgical Australia
55 Clarence St Sydney 2000 Box 3023 GPO Sydney 2001

Concordat cum originali: John P. Dewis
Nihil obstat: Anton Cowan
Imprimatur: Mgr Ralph Brown, VG
    Westminster, 28 June 1982

Approved by the Australian Episcopal Liturgical Commission
Concordat cum originali: Denis J. Hart
Imprimatur: James Cardinal Freeman,
           Archbishop of Sydney
    23 June 1982

© compilation 1982 William Collins Sons & Co Ltd.
ISBN 0 00 599699 6
First published 1982

Acknowledgements

Grateful acknowledgement is made to the following owners of copyright
material for permission to reprint in this volume:
Introductory dialogue and antiphons from *The Divine Office* © 1974 the hierarchies
of England and Wales, Ireland, Australia
Text of psalms from *The Psalms: a new translation* © The Grail (England) 1963
and published by Collins
Text of Canticles Revelation 19:1, 2, 5-7 and 1 Peter 2:21-24 from the
Revised Standard Version Common Bible © 1973 by the Division of
Christian Education, National Council of Churches of Christ in the USA
Text of Magnificat, © 1963 The Grail (England)
M Beattie SJ, words 50
Geoffrey Chapman, a division of Cassell Ltd, for James Quinn SJ, *New Hymns
for All Seasons*, words 38, 39
Timothy Dudley-Smith, words 51 (excluding doxology)
H C A Gaunt, words 44
Paul Inwood, words 55; doxology 49, 51; harmonisation 1, 33, 34, 35, 55
Peter Jones, music 57
Christopher Walker, melody 33
E.J. Warner SJ and Ursuline sisters, Wimbledon, words 52
Roger Williams, music 32
Maurice A Wood, words 42, 43

Sources of music

2 J. Jones (adapted)
3 R.P. Goodenough (adapted)
4 Gregory (adapted)
5 E.J. Hopkins (adapted)
6 T.A. Walmisley (adapted)
7 J. Goss (adapted)
8, 19, 25 J. Randall (adapted)
9, 12, 14, 17, 20, 23, 26, 29 J. Barnby (adapted)
10, 15, 21, 27 T. Jackson (adapted)
11, 16, 22, 28 H. Bishop (adapted)
13, 18, 24, 30 adapted from 'Cambridge Chant'
31 after Dvorak
32 Roger Williams
33 Melody Christopher Walker. Harmonisation Paul Inwood

34, 35 Adapted from plainchant
37, 38, 39 Melody from J.R. Ahle. Harmonisation J.S. Bach
    (Liebster Jesu)
40, 41 C. Ett *(Ave maris stella)*
45, 46 C.F. Witt *(Stuttgart)*
47 Melody, H. Lindenborn. Harmonisation J. Richardson
    (St Bernard)
48 George A. MacFarren
49 Melody T. Haweis. Harmonisation S. Webbe *(Richmond)*
50 O. Gibbons *(Song 46)*
51 W. Greatorex *(Woodlands)*
52 P. Warlock *(Capriol Suite)*
54 Mt Melleray Abbey

Printed and bound in Great Britain by
Collins, Glasgow